Congratulations
Alison & Paul

Cl Heather & Dan

It's a Boy!

by
Marianne Richmond

It's a Boy!

Baby toes photo (page 2) by Lisa Bosman. ljbosman@pressenter.com

Marianne Richmond Studios, Inc.
420 N. 5th Street, Suite 840
Minneapolis, MN 55401
www.mariannerichmond.com

ISBN 0-9753528-3-0

Illustrations by Marianne Richmond

Book design by Sara Dare Biscan

Printed in China

First Printing

TO

FROM

Date

It's a boy!

What an incredible joy.

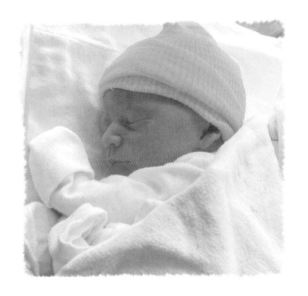

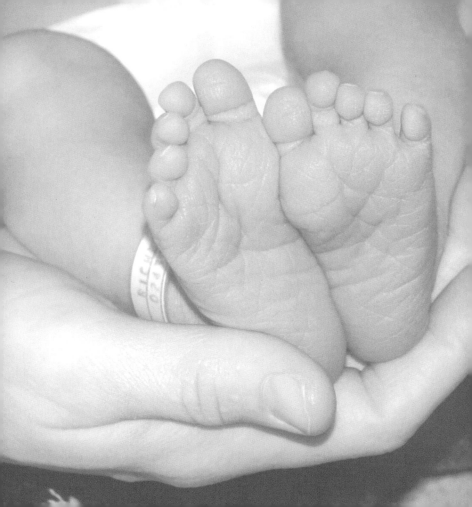

His ten tiny
fingers,
sweet kissable
toes,
chubby cherubic
cheeks,
and cute button
nose.

Did you ever
think someone
so little could
make you feel
love so big?

Delight
in the
"boy-ness"
of
it all.

Baby blue sleepers.
Miniature overalls.

Dots, stripes and plaids.
Cars, trucks and balls.

There is nothing so innocent...
so heartwarming...
as little boy adventures.

Chasing frogs.
Looking for caterpillars.

And playing in anything
muddy or "puddle-y."

He'll endear you with his
crazy colicky hair,
scrapes, bumps and bruises,
Kool Aid® kisses
and everyday muses.

Boys

love

speed.

From crawling to walking.
  From running to riding.
From taking the dare...
  to dare devil.

Hold your breath.

Boys are tough

on the outside.

And so soft

on the inside.

Make time for him.
Listen to him.
Celebrate him.

Kiss him often.

Hug him tightly.

(...but not in front
of his friends!)

And love him unconditionally.

Teach him
kindness
and
manners
and
feelings
and
self sufficiency.

Make time for the important stuff:

Collecting rocks.

Underdogs.

Mud pies.

Freeze tag.

Drawing on the sidewalk.

Making a wish.

Climbing trees.

(If your flexibility allows!)

Boys do cry.

And it's a
good thing.

It shows they are
complex and sensitive
and...

not so tough
after all.

Cherish the journey and
the adventure of parenthood.

The gifts will be many;

the lessons innumerable;

the love all consuming.

It's a boy!

What an
incredible
joy.

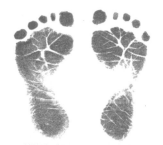

A gifted author and artist, Marianne Richmond shares
her creations with millions of people worldwide
through her delightful books, cards, and giftware.
In addition to the *Simply Said...* and *Smartly Said...*
gift book series, she has written and illustrated four
additional books: **The Gift of an Angel,
The Gift of a Memory, Hooray for You!** and
The Gifts of Being Grand.

To learn more about Marianne's products, please visit
www.mariannerichmond.com.